Josue Tsheleka

Impact of an IT Audit in a Microfinance Institution

Josue Tsheleka

Impact of an IT Audit in a Microfinance Institution

ScienciaScripts

Imprint

Cover image: www.ingimage.com

This book is a translation from the original published under ISBN 978-3-639-62194-5.

Publisher:
Sciencia Scripts
is a trademark of
Dodo Books Indian Ocean Ltd. and OmniScriptum S.R.L publishing group

120 High Road, East Finchley, London, N2 9ED, United Kingdom
Str. Armeneasca 28/1, office 1, Chisinau MD-2012, Republic of Moldova, Europe
Managing Directors: Ieva Konstantinova, Victoria Ursu
info@omniscriptum.com

Printed at: see last page
ISBN: 978-620-8-61939-8

EPIGRAPH

If the world knew how hard I've worked to develop this talent, they wouldn't be surprised.

By Zig Ziglar

"It's smarter to light a tiny lamp, than to complain about the dark."
Lao-Tseu

DEDICATION

All honour to the Lord, our mark of gratitude, honour and love goes straight to God.

To my dearest wife Chancelvie BAKENGA MAMPUYA

To my Champions : Jograce TSHELEKA and Jocha MIJI.

To my dear father Dominique MIJI for his love throughout my studies. It was he who encouraged me in the face of challenge and taught me the terms of existence, of wanting, of well-being, You are the symbol of success.

To my mother Agnès MULENGA for her patience, you were the light of my path. You will always remain in my eyes the symbol of sacrifice. "May God grant you happiness, good health and long life, and help me to be able to light your future and live up to your love for me".

To my only big brother MIJI KANYIMBU Caleb, many have their big brothers but for me he is a divine one. The hard moments and strategies were overcome with

To my Uncles Robert KAWISA, Jean-Luc MUKALAY

To my maternal aunts, MONGA BIBIKAWA and DENISE BUYAMBA, to whom I will always be grateful.

To my paternal aunts MBAMBA SEYA and MARIE KAHINDA for their encouragement and moral support.

I can't repay you for all the happiness you've given me, and I can't value the efforts and sacrifices you've made to achieve this success.

I dedicate this work

Josué TSHELEKA UPALE

INTRODUCTION

For many years now, and increasingly so, the digital environment has played a major role in most organisations. **Production processes, customer relationship management**, the **working environment**: almost everything is now controlled by IT.

The benefits of IT also come with their share of risks, with possible **failures** that could jeopardise all or part of the business (breakdowns, malicious attacks, bad practices that could cause data leaks, etc.).

The information system can be inspected to guard against potential weaknesses. The aim of the audit is to check practices, equipment and data storage (both internal and external).

1. Presentation of microfinance and its role in economic development

a. Presentation of Microfinance

Microfinance is a financial sector that provides financial services to people on low incomes or excluded from traditional banking systems. These services include loans, savings, insurance and money transfers. Microfinance institutions (MFIs) work mainly with people who do not have access to traditional banking services because of their low income, lack of collateral or geographical location.

b. The role of microfinance in economic development

1. **Poverty reduction**: By offering financial services to low-income people, microfinance enables them to start up or expand their economic activities. This can increase their income and improve their standard of living. For example, a micro-loan may enable a person to start a small business, buy equipment or store products.
2. **Promoting financial inclusion**: Microfinance contributes to financial inclusion by giving previously excluded populations access to financial services. This includes not only loans, but also savings accounts, insurance and money transfer services. Financial inclusion is essential for economic development, as it enables more people to participate actively in the economy.
3. **Empowering women**: Many MFIs specifically target women, who make up a large proportion of microfinance clients. By accessing financial services, women can develop their entrepreneurial skills, increase their income and make more autonomous economic decisions for their families.

4. **Support for micro-entrepreneurs**: Micro-entrepreneurs are often the main beneficiaries of microfinance services. These entrepreneurs create jobs not only for themselves, but also for others in their community. By supporting micro-entrepreneurs, microfinance contributes to job creation and local economic growth.
5. **Stimulation of the local economy**: By promoting access to credit and other financial services, microfinance stimulates local economic activity.

Microentrepreneurs invest in their businesses, leading to increased production, sales and consumption in the community.
In short, microfinance plays a crucial role in economic development by offering financial opportunities to people excluded from traditional banking systems. It promotes financial inclusion, reduces poverty, empowers women and supports micro-entrepreneurs, thereby contributing to economic growth and the sustainable development of communities.

2. Definition of an IT audit and its importance

a. Definition of IT Audit

An IT audit is a systematic process for gathering and evaluating evidence about an organisation's information systems and technology infrastructure. Its main objective is to ensure that these systems operate efficiently, reliably and in compliance with current standards and regulations. The IT audit covers various aspects, such as systems security, risk management, data integrity, systems performance and compliance with internal and external policies.

b. Importance of the IT Audit

1. **Systems security**: An IT audit identifies vulnerabilities and security gaps in an organisation's information systems. By detecting these gaps, the audit helps prevent cyber-attacks, data breaches and other security incidents that could compromise sensitive information and the organisation's reputation.
2. **Risk management**: The IT audit assesses the risks associated with information technology and proposes measures to mitigate them. This includes assessing the risks associated with software, hardware, networks and IT processes. Effective risk management minimises disruption and potential financial loss.
3. **Regulatory compliance**: Many industries are subject to strict data protection and IT security regulations. The IT audit ensures that the organisation complies with these legal and regulatory requirements, avoiding financial penalties and reputational damage.
4. **Data integrity**: The IT audit verifies the accuracy, completeness and reliability of data processed by information systems. This ensures that the information used to make strategic decisions is reliable and free from error or fraudulent manipulation.
5. **Operational efficiency**: The IT audit assesses the performance of IT systems and processes. By identifying inefficiencies and bottlenecks, the audit helps to optimise IT resources and improve the overall efficiency of the organisation.
6. **Business planning and continuity**: The IT audit examines the organisation's disaster recovery and contingency plans. It ensures that

the necessary measures are in place to guarantee business continuity in the event of a disaster or major breakdown.

In short, IT auditing is essential to guarantee the security, reliability and efficiency of an organisation's information systems. It plays a crucial role in risk management, regulatory compliance, data integrity and improving operational performance.

CHAPTER 1: MICROFINANCE AND ITS IMPORTANCE

1. History and development of microfinance

Microfinance has a rich and diverse history, dating back centuries in some forms, but really consolidating itself as a global movement over the last few decades. Here is an overview of its history and evolution:

The first forms of microfinance

- **18th century:** The first forms of microfinance can be traced back to community banks and cooperative credit associations in Europe. For example, the Caisses Raiffeisen in Germany, founded by Friedrich Wilhelm Raiffeisen in the 1860s, offered financial services to poor farmers.
- **1970s**: Modern microfinance begins to take shape. In 1976, Muhammad Yunus, a professor of economics in Bangladesh, founded the Grameen Bank. The Grameen Bank model is based on granting small unsecured loans to poor entrepreneurs, mainly women, to help them start up or expand their small businesses. This model proves that poor people can be reliable borrowers when they are supported by appropriate structures.

The Emergence of Modern Microfinance

- **1980s-1990s:** Microfinance expands rapidly. Microfinance institutions (MFIs) are set up all over the world, adopting and adapting the Grameen Bank model. During this period, organisations such as ACCION International, FINCA and BRAC also play a key role in promoting microfinance.
- **2000s:** Microfinance continues to develop and evolve. MFIs begin to diversify their products and services to include not only loans, but also savings accounts, insurance and money transfer services. Technology also plays an increasingly important role, with the introduction of digital microfinance and mobile banking.

The Impact of Microfinance

- **Nobel Peace Prize 2006:** Muhammad Yunus and the Grameen Bank receive the Nobel Peace Prize for their efforts to create economic and social development from the ground up. This prize highlights microfinance and its potential to combat poverty.
- **Recent developments :** Today, microfinance continues to transform. Technological innovations, such as peer-to-peer (P2P) lending platforms and FinTech solutions, offer new opportunities and challenges for the sector. Microfinance is also expanding to new markets and population segments, including young entrepreneurs and rural populations.

Challenges and opportunities

- **Challenges:** Despite its successes, microfinance faces a number of challenges, such as the financial sustainability of MFIs, risk management and regulation.

The issue of high interest rates in some microfinance programmes is also the subject of debate.

- **Opportunities:** Microfinance continues to play a crucial role in financial inclusion and economic development. Technological advances and the integration of digital financial services offer opportunities to reach even more people excluded from traditional financial systems.

  In short, microfinance has come a long way from its earliest community-based forms to become a powerful instrument for poverty reduction and financial inclusion. Its continuing evolution is testament to its resilience and ability to adapt to the changing needs of low-income populations.

2. The main players in the microfinance sector1

Here are some of the main players in the microfinance sector worldwide:

1. **Grameen Bank**: Founded by Muhammad Yunus in Bangladesh, this institution is often regarded as the pioneer of modern microfinance.
2. **FINCA International**: A global organisation providing financial services to vulnerable communities in over 20 countries.
3. **Accion**: An international organisation that helps people out of poverty through tailored financial services.
4. **BRAC**: An organisation based in Bangladesh that offers a wide range of services, including microfinance, to improve the living conditions of low-income people.
5. **BancoSol**: A bank in Bolivia that focuses on providing financial services to micro-entrepreneurs and small businesses.
6. **La Nef**: A financial cooperative in France offering solidarity financing, loans and savings to support projects with a social and environmental impact.
7. **Adie**: A French association that grants microcredits and helps people excluded from the traditional banking system to set up their own business.
8. **SKS Microfinance**: A microfinance institution in India which was one of the largest in the world before its transformation into a commercial bank.
9. **SM GUILGAL SA**: A microfinance institution in the DRC which is one of the largest in the country and supports people excluded from the banking system.

These players play a crucial role in promoting financial inclusion and supporting micro-entrepreneurs, thereby contributing to poverty reduction and economic development in their respective communities.

[1] www.falcinvest.com

3. The challenges and opportunities of microfinance

Challenges and opportunities for microfinance

Challenges

1. **Financial sustainability**: Many microfinance institutions (MFIs) depend on subsidies and donations to operate. Finding a business model that is sustainable while remaining accessible to low-income clients is a major challenge.
2. **High interest rates**: Some MFIs charge high interest rates to compensate for risks and operational costs, which can put additional financial pressure on borrowers.
3. **Risk of over-indebtedness**: Borrowers may find themselves with several simultaneous loans, leading to an increased risk of over-indebtedness. This can affect their ability to repay and compromise their financial situation.
4. **Regulatory compliance**: MFIs have to navigate often complex and changing regulatory environments. Complying with local and international regulations can be a major challenge.
5. **Limited financial inclusion**: Despite progress, a large proportion of the world's population remains excluded from financial services. MFIs need to find innovative ways to reach the unreached, particularly in rural areas.
6. **Technological issues**: Integrating modern technologies into microfinance operations can be costly and complex, especially for small MFIs with limited resources.

Opportunities

1. **Financial inclusion**: Microfinance offers significant opportunities for financial inclusion, by providing financial services to populations that were previously excluded. This can help to reduce poverty and improve economic well-being.
2. **Empowerment of women**: MFIs that target women contribute to their economic empowerment. By accessing financial services, women can undertake business, save and invest in their families' education and health.
3. **Technological innovation**: Technological advances, such as mobile banking and FinTech platforms, offer opportunities to improve the efficiency and accessibility of microfinance services. These innovations can reduce operational costs and improve the user experience.
4. **Product diversification**: MFIs can diversify their offerings to include insurance products, money transfer services and savings programmes. This helps to meet the varied financial needs of customers and improve their economic resilience.
5. **Social and environmental impact**: MFIs have the opportunity to support projects with a positive social and environmental impact. For example, they can finance sustainable agricultural initiatives or renewable energy projects in rural communities.
6. **Partnerships and collaborations**: MFIs can collaborate with governments, NGOs and businesses to extend their reach and maximise their impact. These

partnerships can provide financial and technical support, as well as training and capacity building opportunities.

In summary, although microfinance faces significant challenges, it also offers many opportunities for financial inclusion, women's empowerment and sustainable economic development. MFIs must continue to innovate and adapt to meet these challenges and seize these opportunities.

CHAPTER 2: THE IT AUDIT: CONCEPTS AND METHODOLOGIES

1. Definition and objectives of an IT audit

Definition of IT Audit

An IT audit is a systematic process of gathering, analysing and evaluating evidence about an organisation's information systems, technology infrastructure and IT operations. The main objective is to ensure that these systems operate efficiently, securely and in compliance with current standards and regulations. The IT audit covers various aspects, such as systems security, risk management, data integrity and systems performance.

Objectives of the IT Audit

1. **Systems security**: Identifying and assessing vulnerabilities in information systems to prevent cyber-attacks, unauthorised access and data breaches.
2. **Risk management**: Assessing the risks associated with information technology and proposing measures to mitigate them, thereby minimising disruption and potential financial loss.
3. **Regulatory compliance**: Ensuring that the organisation complies with laws, regulations and internal policies on data protection and IT security, thereby avoiding financial penalties and reputational damage.
4. **Data integrity:** Checking the accuracy, completeness and reliability of data processed by information systems, thereby ensuring that the information used to make strategic decisions is reliable.
5. **Operational efficiency:** Evaluate the performance of IT systems and processes to identify inefficiencies and bottlenecks, enabling resources to be optimised and the overall efficiency of the organisation to be improved.
6. **Business continuity planning:** Review the organisation's disaster recovery and contingency plans to ensure that the necessary measures are in place to guarantee business continuity in the event of a major disaster or breakdown.

In short, IT audit plays a crucial role in protecting and improving an organisation's information systems. It helps to manage risk, guarantee regulatory compliance, ensure data integrity and optimise operational performance.

2. The different IT audit methods

IT audit methods are varied and adapted to the specific objectives of each audit. Here are some of the main methods used:

1. Compliance audit

- **Objective**: To check that information systems comply with laws, regulations and internal policies.
- **Methods** :
  - Review of internal policies and procedures

- Checking system configurations
- Compliance checks

2. Security audit

- **Objective**: Identify and assess vulnerabilities in information systems to prevent cyber attacks and data breaches.
- **Methods** :
    - Penetration tests (pentests)
    - Vulnerability analysis
    - Review of security logs
    - Assessment of access controls

3. Performance audit

- **Objective**: To assess the effectiveness and efficiency of information systems.
- **Methods** :
    - Load and stress tests
    - Network performance analysis
    - Review of application response times
    - Assessment of capacity and use of resources

4. Risk management audit

- **Objective**: Identify and assess the risks associated with information technology and propose measures to mitigate them.
- **Methods** :
    - Risk analysis
    - Assessment of internal controls
    - Review of risk management processes
    - Interviews with key personnel

5. Audit of IT processes

- **Objective**: To assess the effectiveness of IT-related processes.
- **Methods** :
    - Review of ITIL (Information Technology Infrastructure Library) processes
    - Workflow analysis
    - Interviews with technical staff
    - Review of process documents and reports

6. Audit of information systems

- **Objective**: To assess the quality, integrity and security of information systems.
- **Methods** :
    - Application testing
    - Review of databases
    - Assessment of system interfaces
    - Data integrity tests

7. Business continuity audit

- **Objective**: To ensure that the necessary measures are in place to guarantee continuity of operations in the event of a disaster or major breakdown.
- **Methods** :
    - Review of disaster recovery plans
    - System restoration tests

- Assessment of business continuity plans
- Crisis scenario simulation

By applying these different methods, IT auditors can obtain a complete and accurate view of the state of an organisation's information systems, identify areas requiring improvement and propose recommendations to optimise security, performance and compliance.

3. Tools and techniques used in IT audits

Tools

1. **Audit management software**
    - *Examples*: ACL, IDEA, Teammate
    - *Benefits*: Automate and facilitate management of the audit process, from planning to report generation.
2. **Safety monitoring tools**
    - *Examples*: Splunk, SIEM (Security Information and Event Management), Snort
    - *Purpose*: Monitor and analyse network activities to detect threats and security incidents.
3. **Vulnerability analysis tools**
    - *Examples*: Nessus, OpenVAS, QualysGuard
    - *What it does*: Scans systems and networks to identify security flaws and vulnerabilities.
4. **Penetration testing tools**
    - *Examples*: Metasploit, Burp Suite, OWASP ZAP
    - *Benefits*: Simulate attacks to assess system security and identify weak points.
5. **Risk management tools**
    - *Examples*: RiskWatch, Resolver, RSA Archer
    - *Benefits*: Assess, monitor and manage IT-related risks.
6. **Data management tools**
    - *Examples*: SQL Server Management Studio (SSMS), Oracle Data Guard, IBM InfoSphere
    - *Utility*: Manage and analyse data stored in databases to ensure their integrity and security.

Techniques

1. **Documentation review**
    - *Description*: Reviews policies, procedures, manuals and other documents to assess the compliance and effectiveness of internal controls.
2. **Interviews**
    - *Description*: Conducts interviews with key personnel to understand processes, identify potential risks and assess the controls in place.
3. **Direct observation**
    - *Description*: Observe operations and processes in real time to assess their compliance and efficiency.
4. **Testing and sampling**
    - *Description*: Carry out tests on samples of data and transactions to check the accuracy, completeness and correctness of information.
5. **Log analysis**
    - *Description*: Examine system and application logs to detect suspicious activity and security incidents.
6. **Configuration analysis**
    - *Description*: Checks system and network configurations to ensure that they comply with security policies and best practice.
7. **Penetration tests (Pentests)**
    - *Description*: Simulate attacks on systems to identify vulnerabilities and assess the robustness of the security measures in place.
8. **Review of access controls**
    - *Description*: Evaluate access control mechanisms to ensure that only authorised users have access to sensitive systems and data.

These tools and techniques enable IT auditors to carry out in-depth and rigorous assessments of information systems, identifying vulnerabilities, evaluating risks and proposing recommendations to improve the security and efficiency of technological infrastructures.

CHAPTER 3: THE IMPACT OF IT AUDIT ON MICROFINANCE OPERATIONS

3.1 Security and data protection

IT audits help to strengthen the security of information systems within microfinance institutions. By identifying and correcting vulnerabilities, MFIs can protect their customers' sensitive data against cyber-attacks, unauthorised access and data loss. Enhanced security helps to maintain customer confidence and ensure business continuity.

Security and data protection are crucial aspects for any organisation, especially microfinance institutions, where sensitive information about customers and financial transactions must be protected. Here are some key points to consider:

1. Security policies

- **Drawing up security policies**: Create clear security policies that all employees can understand, to define the rules and expected behaviour when it comes to data management.
- **Employee training**: Regularly train staff in security best practice and make them aware of the risks associated with cyber attacks and data breaches.

2. Access controls

- **Strong authentication**: Implement multi-factor authentication mechanisms to ensure that only authorised people have access to sensitive systems and data.
- **Identity and access management**: Using tools to manage and control user access to different IT resources, assigning access rights according to individual roles and responsibilities.

3. Data encryption

- **Encryption of data in transit**: Use encryption protocols, such as SSL/TLS, to protect data as it is transmitted over networks.
- **Encryption of data at rest**: Encrypt data stored on servers, databases and storage devices to prevent unauthorised access in the event of theft or loss of hardware.

4. Threat monitoring and detection

- **Intrusion Detection Systems (IDS) and Intrusion Prevention Systems (IPS)**: Install IDS/IPS solutions to monitor networks and systems, detect suspicious activity and prevent attacks in real time.
- **Log analysis**: collect and analyse system and application logs to identify anomalous behaviour and unauthorised access attempts.

5. Data backup and restoration

- **Backup planning**: Implement regular backup procedures to ensure that data can be restored in the event of loss, corruption or cyber-attack.
- **Restoration tests**: Carry out regular restoration tests on backups to ensure that data can be recovered reliably and quickly.

6. **Regulatory compliance**

- **Regulatory compliance**: Ensure that data security practices comply with local and international regulations, such as the General Data Protection Regulation (GDPR) in Europe.
- **Audit and assessment**: Carry out regular audits to assess compliance with security policies and identify areas requiring improvement.

By implementing these measures, microfinance institutions can strengthen data security and protection, reduce the risk of cyber attacks and maintain the trust of their customers. Data security is an ongoing responsibility that requires constant vigilance and adaptation to new threats and technologies.

3.2 Improving operational processes

With an IT audit, MFIs can identify inefficiencies and bottlenecks in their operational processes. By implementing the audit recommendations, they can optimise their workflows, reduce operational costs and improve the quality of their services. The result is greater customer satisfaction and increased competitiveness.

IT audit plays a crucial role in improving the operational processes of microfinance institutions. By identifying inefficiencies and bottlenecks, IT auditors can propose recommendations to optimise workflows, reduce operational costs and improve the quality of services offered. Here are some of the ways in which IT auditing can improve business processes:

1. **Process automation**

- **Benefit**: Automating repetitive and manual tasks saves time, reduces human error and improves overall efficiency.
- **Example**: Implementation of automated systems for processing loan applications, managing customer accounts and generating financial reports.

2. **Workflow optimisation**

- **Benefit**: By assessing existing processes, IT auditors can identify bottlenecks and suggest improvements to optimise workflows.
- **Example**: Reorganisation of loan processing stages to reduce processing times and improve customer satisfaction.

3. **Improving data quality**

- **Benefit**: Data quality is essential for making informed and effective decisions. An IT audit verifies data integrity and accuracy.
- **Example**: Implementation of data quality controls and data cleansing procedures to ensure that the information used is reliable and accurate.

4. **Resource management**

- **Advantage**: The IT audit helps to identify under-utilised or inefficient resources and proposes solutions to optimise their use.

- **Example**: Redistributing IT resources to ensure they are used optimally and meet operational needs.

5. Reducing operating costs

- **Benefit**: By identifying inefficiencies and proposing optimisation solutions, the IT audit helps to reduce operational costs.
- **Example**: Adoption of more efficient and less costly technologies, such as cloud computing, to reduce expenditure on hardware and maintenance.

6. Improving communication and collaboration

- **Advantage**: The IT audit can reveal shortcomings in communication and collaboration within the organisation and propose solutions to improve them.
- **Example**: Setting up online collaboration platforms and communication tools to facilitate information sharing and coordination between teams.

7. Implementing best practice

- **Benefit**: Based on industry best practice, IT auditors can recommend improvements that align operational processes with high performance and security standards.
- **Example**: Adoption of quality and security management frameworks, such as ITIL (Information Technology Infrastructure Library) and ISO 27001, to ensure operational excellence.

By implementing the recommendations arising from IT audits, microfinance institutions can not only improve their operational processes, but also strengthen their resilience, increase their efficiency and offer better quality services to their customers. Optimising operational processes is a key lever for the competitiveness and sustainable growth of MFIs.

3.3 Regulatory compliance and risk reduction

IT audits help MFIs comply with current regulations and standards on data protection and IT security. By ensuring compliance, they can avoid financial penalties and damage to their reputation. In addition, the audit helps to detect and manage potential risks, thereby contributing to the stability and resilience of the institution.

1. Regulatory compliance

Ensuring compliance with current laws and regulations is essential for microfinance institutions. Non-compliance can lead to financial penalties, loss of reputation and legal risks. Here are some key aspects of regulatory compliance:

- **Identification of applicable regulations**: MFIs should identify and understand the local and international regulations that apply to their operations. This may include regulations on data protection, anti-money laundering (AML), IT security, and lending practices.
- **Implementation of policies and procedures**: Develop and implement internal policies and procedures to ensure that all operations comply with applicable regulations. These policies should be clearly documented and communicated to all staff.

- **Training and awareness**: Regularly train employees on regulatory requirements and internal policies. Awareness-raising is essential to ensure that everyone in the organisation understands and complies with regulations.
- **Compliance audits**: Carry out regular compliance audits to assess the institution's level of compliance and identify areas requiring improvement. These audits may be carried out internally or by external experts.

2. Risk Reduction

Effective risk management is crucial to the stability and resilience of microfinance institutions. Here are some strategies for reducing risk:

- **Risk identification and assessment**: Identifying potential risks associated with information technology and microfinance operations. Assess these risks in terms of their likelihood and impact.
- **Development of internal controls**: Implementing internal controls to mitigate identified risks. This may include security controls, transaction verification procedures and activity monitoring mechanisms.
- **Business continuity planning**: Draw up business continuity and disaster recovery plans to ensure that the institution can continue to operate in the event of a disaster or major breakdown. These plans should include procedures for backing up data and restoring systems.
- **Ongoing monitoring and evaluation**: Implement ongoing monitoring mechanisms to detect emerging risks and evaluate the effectiveness of internal controls. MFIs must be proactive in risk management by adapting their strategies in line with new threats and regulatory changes.
- **Working with experts**: Work with risk management and compliance experts to benefit from their knowledge and advice. Experts can help identify best practice and implement effective solutions to reduce risk.

By implementing these strategies, microfinance institutions can ensure that they comply with current regulations and reduce the risks associated with their operations. Regulatory compliance and risk management are essential to the sustainability and success of MFIs, contributing to customer confidence and the stability of the sector.

3.4 Case study of a microfinance institution that carried out an IT audit[2]

To illustrate the impact of the IT audit, let's take the example of a fictitious microfinance institution, "MicroFinancePlus". Prior to the audit, MicroFinancePlus was facing security challenges, operational inefficiencies and regulatory compliance issues. After hiring a team of IT auditors, the institution was able to :

- Identify and correct critical security vulnerabilities.
- Optimise lending and customer account management processes.
- Implement robust internal controls to ensure regulatory compliance.
- Reduce operational risks and improve the resilience of the organisation.

[2] www.academia.edu

As a result, MicroFinancePlus has seen an increase in customer satisfaction, a reduction in operating costs and an improvement in its reputation in the market.

A notable example of a microfinance institution that has implemented an IT audit is **Credit Mutuel du Sénégal (CMS)**. This institution carried out a credit risk management study using IT audit methods to improve its processes and reduce losses linked to unpaid loans1.

Case study: Credit Mutuel du Sénégal (CMS)

Context

Credit Mutuel du Sénégal (CMS) is a microfinance institution that implemented an IT audit to evaluate and improve its credit risk management processes. The main objective was to reduce losses linked to unpaid loans and improve the institution's financial health1.

Methodology

The CMS IT audit involved two main phases:

1. **Analysis of the customer's character**: This phase consisted of using the data collected during the interviews to assess the customer's reliability and solvency.
2. **Analysis of the customer's financial health**: This phase involved using financial and accounting data to assess the customer's financial situation.

Results

Thanks to the IT audit, the CMS was able to :

- **Reducing the rate of unpaid loans**: Using financial diagnostic methods, the institution was able to identify potential risks and grant loans only to customers with a good repayment history.
- **Improving risk management**: The audit led to the implementation of more robust internal controls to mitigate credit risks.
- **Optimising resources**: By identifying inefficiencies and proposing optimisation solutions, the institution has been able to reduce its operating costs and improve overall efficiency.

The CMS IT audit demonstrated the importance of using advanced technologies and methodologies to improve the risk management and financial performance of microfinance institutions. This approach has enabled CMS to strengthen its financial stability and better serve its customers.

This example shows how IT audit can be a powerful tool for microfinance institutions, enabling them to make more informed decisions and reduce the risks associated with their operations.

Conclusion: IT audit plays a crucial role in improving the security, efficiency and compliance of microfinance institutions. By adopting audit recommendations, MFIs can build resilience, protect customer data and deliver better quality services. The positive impact of the IT audit translates into greater customer confidence, increased competitiveness and a significant contribution to economic development.

CHAPTER 4: CHALLENGES AND LIMITATIONS OF IT AUDIT IN MICROFINANCE

4.1 Cost and resource issues

IT audits can be expensive, particularly for small microfinance institutions with limited resources. The costs include not only the auditors' fees, but also the expenses associated with implementing the recommendations. In addition, MFIs may not have qualified staff in-house to carry out audits, so external consultants have to be hired.

Microfinance institutions (MFIs) can face a number of challenges in terms of the costs and resources required to carry out IT audits. Here are some of the main issues:

1. Audit costs

- **Auditors' fees**: Hiring IT audit experts can be expensive, especially if the institution has to use external consultants. Fees vary according to the complexity and scope of the audit.
- **Tools and technologies** : The tools and software required to conduct effective IT audits can represent a significant investment. MFIs often need to invest in cutting-edge technology to ensure the accuracy and completeness of audits.
- **Staff training**: Training employees in IT audit best practice and in the use of specific tools can also generate costs. Regular training is necessary to keep skills up to date with technological developments.

2. Human resources

- **Availability of experts**: Finding qualified IT audit experts can be a challenge, especially in regions where these skills are in short supply. A lack of qualified personnel can delay audits and affect their quality.
- **Workload**: IT audits can be lengthy and complex, requiring significant involvement from internal teams. This can overload existing staff and affect other critical operations.
- **Outsourcing**: To compensate for the lack of in-house resources, some MFIs choose to outsource their IT audits to specialist companies. While this can guarantee quality expertise, it can also lead to additional costs and coordination challenges.

3. Initial investment and maintenance

- **Initial investment**: Implementing the infrastructure required for IT audits requires a significant initial investment. MFIs need to allocate substantial budgets for the purchase of hardware, software and the implementation of processes.
- **Maintenance costs**: Maintaining and updating IT audit tools and systems requires ongoing resources. MFIs should budget for regular maintenance, software updates and technical support.

4. Adapting to technological change

- **Technological developments**: Audit technologies and methodologies are evolving rapidly. MFIs must constantly adapt to new trends and best practices, which can represent a challenge in terms of costs and resources.

- **Obsolescence of tools**: The tools and technologies used for IT audits can become obsolete, requiring regular investment in new solutions.

Solutions and recommendations

To overcome these challenges, here are some recommendations for MFIs:

1. **Budget planning**: Allocate specific budgets for IT audits, taking into account initial costs and maintenance costs. Rigorous financial planning can help to better manage expenditure.
2. **Ongoing training**: Invest in ongoing staff training to keep skills up to date and ensure in-house expertise in IT auditing.
3. **Strategic partnerships**: Establish partnerships with companies specialising in IT auditing to benefit from their expertise while optimising costs.
4. **Use of open source solutions**: Consider using open source software to reduce licence and subscription costs.
5. **Modular approach**: Adopt a modular approach to IT audits, focusing initially on critical areas and gradually extending audits to other sectors.

By implementing these strategies, MFIs can more effectively manage the challenges associated with the costs and resources required for IT audits, while guaranteeing the security and efficiency of their operations.

4.2 Resistance to change and cultural challenges

MFI employees and management may be reluctant to accept changes recommended by IT auditors. This resistance to change may be due to fear of the unknown, concerns about job security or a rigid organisational culture. It is essential to educate and train staff to overcome these barriers.

Microfinance institutions (MFIs) can encounter resistance to change and cultural challenges when undertaking IT audits or adopting new technologies. Here are some of the main issues and recommendations for overcoming them:

1. Resistance to change

- **Fears and concerns**: Employees may fear that IT audits and new technologies will jeopardise their job security or change their responsibilities. This fear of the unknown can lead to passive or active resistance.
- **Lack of confidence**: Employees may lack confidence in management or in the need for the proposed changes. They may perceive audits as a criticism of their work rather than a tool for improvement.
- **Entrenched habits**: Employees may be reluctant to give up their tried and tested ways of working and adopt new practices, even if these are more efficient.

2. Cultural challenges

- **Differences in perception**: Different stakeholders may have different perceptions and expectations of IT technologies and audits. This can lead to misunderstandings and conflicts.
- **Organisational culture**: Some organisations have a rigid culture that values the status quo and resists change. In such cultures, it can be difficult to introduce new ideas and practices.
- **Inadequate communication**: A lack of clear and transparent communication about the reasons for and benefits of IT audits can reinforce resistance and cultural challenges.

Solutions and recommendations

1. **Communication and awareness-raising**
    - **Inform and educate**: Organise information and training sessions to explain the objectives, benefits and implications of IT audits. Use concrete examples to illustrate how these changes can improve processes and results.
    - **Transparency**: Communicate transparently about the reasons for the changes and how they will be implemented. Involve employees from the outset to gather their opinions and suggestions.
2. **Employee involvement and commitment**
    - **Active participation**: Involve employees in the change process by encouraging them to participate actively in discussions, decisions and the implementation of new practices.
    - **Recognition and Reward**: Recognise and reward employees who positively embrace change and contribute to its success. This can motivate others to follow their example.
3. **Training and Skills Development**
    - **Ongoing training**: Providing ongoing training to develop employees' technical skills and knowledge of IT technologies and audits. Provide support to facilitate adaptation to new practices.
    - **Technical Support**: Set up technical support teams to help employees solve problems and overcome technical obstacles.
4. **Leadership and Culture of Change**
    - **Inspirational Leadership**: Leaders must set an example by embracing change and demonstrating their commitment to continuous improvement. They must also actively support employees throughout the process.
    - **Culture of Change**: Promote an organisational culture that values innovation, continuous learning and adaptability. Encourage employees to propose ideas and experiment with new approaches.

5. **Progressive Approach**
    - **Step-by-step implementation** : Adopt a phased approach to implementing IT audits and new technologies. Start with pilot projects to test and adjust practices before rolling them out on a large scale.
    - **Evaluation and Adjustment**: Regularly evaluate the impact of changes and adjust strategies based on feedback. Involve employees in this evaluation process to ensure that they feel heard and taken into account.

By proactively addressing resistance to change and cultural challenges, microfinance institutions can facilitate the adoption of IT audits and new technologies, thereby strengthening their effectiveness and resilience. Transparent communication, employee engagement and ongoing support are essential for a successful transition.

4.3 Technical and infrastructure problems

MFIs operating in remote or underdeveloped regions may encounter technical and infrastructure problems, such as unstable Internet connections, frequent power outages and lack of access to advanced technologies. These challenges can limit the effectiveness of the IT audit and complicate the implementation of recommendations.

Microfinance institutions (MFIs) can encounter technical and infrastructure challenges when trying to adopt IT audits and new technologies. Here are some of the main issues and potential solutions to overcome them:

1. Unstable Internet connections

- **Problem**: In many rural or remote areas, Internet connections can be unstable or non-existent, making it difficult to access the online tools and resources needed for IT audits.
- **Solution**: Invest in alternative solutions such as satellite connections or 4G/5G mobile networks. MFIs can also use offline audit tools that allow data to be collected and analysed without an Internet connection, with subsequent synchronisation when the connection is available.

2. Frequent power failures

- **Problem**: Frequent power failures can interrupt audit processes and compromise data integrity.
- **Solution**: Install uninterruptible power supplies (UPS) and generators to ensure continuity of power supply. MFIs can also consider using renewable energy sources such as solar panels to reduce their dependence on unstable electricity grids.

3. Lack of access to advanced technologies

- **Problem**: MFIs may not have access to the advanced technologies needed to carry out effective IT audits, due to high costs or geographical limitations.
- **Solution**: Work with technology partners to obtain subsidies, loans or donations of equipment. MFIs can also explore options for leasing or renting

technology equipment to reduce initial costs. Using open source solutions and free software can also be a viable alternative.

4. System compatibility problems

- **Problem**: Existing information systems may be incompatible with new IT audit tools, making data integration and analysis difficult.
- **Solution**: Carry out a thorough assessment of existing systems before adopting new tools. Choose modular and flexible solutions that can be easily integrated into existing systems. Work with technology suppliers to develop specific compatibility interfaces.

5. Ageing infrastructure

- **Problem**: Ageing IT infrastructures may not be able to support new audit tools and technologies, limiting their effectiveness.
- **Solution**: Regularly plan and budget for the updating and renewal of IT infrastructures. Prioritise investment in the most critical areas to ensure that the infrastructure remains robust and capable of meeting current and future needs.

6. Lack of technical skills

- **Problem**: A lack of technical skills within the organisation can hinder the adoption and effective use of IT audits and new technologies.
- **Solution**: Invest in staff training and technical skills development. Recruit external experts to fill skills gaps and provide mentoring to internal employees. Encourage a culture of continuous learning to keep skills up to date.

By overcoming these technical and infrastructure challenges, microfinance institutions can take full advantage of IT audits to improve operations, strengthen data security and ensure regulatory compliance. A proactive approach and strategic investments are essential to meet these challenges and ensure the long-term success of MFIs.

4.4 Complexity of information systems

MFIs' information systems can be complex and varied, with multiple integrations and legacy processes. This complexity makes IT auditing more difficult, as auditors have to understand and assess heterogeneous systems. In addition, systems documentation may be insufficient or obsolete, further complicating the audit.

The information systems of microfinance institutions (MFIs) can be very complex, due to the diversity of technologies used, multiple integrations and legacy processes. This complexity can pose a number of challenges during an IT audit. Here are some of the main problems linked to the complexity of information systems and solutions to overcome them:

1. Diversity of technologies

- **Problem**: MFIs often use a combination of old and new technologies, which can complicate the IT audit. Auditors need to understand and assess a variety of systems, from relational databases to cloud computing applications.

- **Solution**: Train IT auditors in a range of technologies and platforms. Use audit tools that can integrate and analyse different types of systems. Collaborate with experts specialised in the specific technologies used by the institution.

2. **Systems integration**

- **Problem**: MFI information systems can be complexly integrated, with data flows between different applications and databases. Auditing these integrations can be difficult due to multiple connection points and dependencies.
- **Solution**: Map system integrations and create data flow diagrams to visualise connections and dependencies. Use integration monitoring tools to detect problems and inefficiencies. Carry out integration tests to ensure that systems are communicating correctly.

3. **Inherited processes**

- **Problem**: MFIs may still be using legacy processes that have not been modernised for a long time. These processes may be poorly documented, difficult to understand and incompatible with new technologies.
- **Solution**: Document and analyse legacy processes to identify inefficiencies and risks. Implement modernisation projects to migrate to more modern and efficient systems and processes. Use change management methodologies to facilitate the transition.

4. **Insufficient or obsolete documentation**

- **Problem**: Information systems documentation may be inadequate, obsolete or non-existent, which complicates IT audits and systems assessment.
- **Solution**: Update and maintain complete and accurate information systems documentation. Use documentation management tools to centralise and organise information. Involve the technical teams in creating and updating documentation.

5. **Safety of complex systems**

- **Problem**: The complexity of systems can make security more difficult to manage. Vulnerabilities can be harder to detect and correct due to multiple layers and integrations.
- **Solution**: Implement robust security controls at every level of the system. Use security monitoring and analysis tools to detect threats and vulnerabilities. Carry out regular security audits to evaluate and reinforce the security of complex systems.

6. **Maintenance and updates**

- **Problem**: Maintaining and updating complex systems can be difficult to manage, due to dependencies and the risk of disrupting operations.
- **Solution**: Plan and coordinate updates and maintenance proactively, minimising interruptions to operations. Use test environments to validate updates before deploying them to production. Implement change management policies to ensure smooth updates and maintenance.

4.5 Varied regulatory compliance

MFIs often operate in multiple jurisdictions, each with its own regulations and compliance standards. Navigating this complex regulatory environment can be a major challenge for IT auditors. Understanding and complying with local and international requirements is essential to avoid penalties and reputational damage.

Here are some of the main problems associated with varied regulatory compliance and solutions to overcome them:

1. Diversity of regulations

- **Issue**: MFIs must comply with national, regional and international regulations which can vary considerably. These regulations can include data protection standards, anti-money laundering (AML) requirements, IT security rules and responsible lending practices.
- **Solution**: Create a dedicated regulatory compliance team to monitor and interpret applicable regulations. Use regulatory monitoring tools to keep abreast of changes and updates to laws and regulations.

2. Interpretation of regulations

- **Problem**: Regulations can be complex and open to interpretation. MFIs may find it difficult to understand how to apply the regulations to their specific operations.
- **Solution**: Work with legal experts and compliance consultants to obtain advice on interpreting regulations. Organise training sessions for employees on regulatory requirements and their practical application.

3. Process harmonisation

- **Problem**: MFIs need to harmonise their internal processes to meet the compliance requirements of different jurisdictions. This can be particularly challenging for institutions operating in multiple countries.
- **Solution**: Implement global compliance policies and procedures that can be adapted to local requirements. Use compliance management tools to centralise and standardise processes.

4. Implementation of controls

- **Issue**: MFIs need to put in place internal controls to ensure that all operations comply with applicable regulations. This may include security controls, transaction verification procedures and activity monitoring mechanisms.
- **Solution**: Use audit and monitoring tools to automate internal controls and ensure their effectiveness. Carry out regular compliance audits to assess compliance with regulations and identify areas requiring improvement.

5. Coordination with regulatory authorities

- **Problem**: MFIs have to coordinate with several regulatory authorities, each with their own requirements and expectations. This can lead to a significant administrative burden and communication challenges.

- **Solution**: Establish strong working relationships with regulators and appoint dedicated contact points to facilitate communication. Participate in compliance forums and working groups to exchange information and best practice.

6. Adapting to regulatory changes

- **Problem**: Regulations can change rapidly, and MFIs need to be able to adapt to these changes to remain compliant.
- **Solution**: Implement a regulatory change management process to monitor updates and adjust policies and procedures accordingly. Regularly train employees on new regulations and changes to existing regulations.

By adopting these strategies, MFIs can manage the diversity of regulations more effectively and ensure compliance in the different jurisdictions in which they operate. A proactive and systematic approach to regulatory compliance is essential to reduce risk and maintain stakeholder confidence.

4.6 Lack of IT audit awareness

In some MFIs, management may not be fully aware of the importance of IT audit. A lack of awareness and understanding can lead to an underestimation of the benefits of audit and limited support for IT audit initiatives. It is crucial to promote an audit culture and make management aware of its benefits.

Awareness of IT auditing is crucial to ensuring the security and efficiency of information systems in microfinance institutions (MFIs). However, lack of awareness can pose a number of challenges. Here are some of the main problems associated with a lack of IT audit awareness and solutions to overcome them:

1. Lack of awareness of the benefits of IT auditing

- **Problem**: Employees and management may not understand the benefits of IT auditing, which can lead to a lack of support and resources for audit initiatives.
- **Solution**: Organise awareness-raising and training sessions to explain the benefits of IT auditing, such as improved security, operational efficiency and regulatory compliance. Use concrete examples and case studies to illustrate these benefits.

2. Low priority given to IT audit

- **Problem**: Without adequate awareness, IT auditing can be perceived as a secondary task to other operational priorities.
- **Solution**: Integrate the IT audit into the organisation's overall strategy and make it a priority for management. Clearly communicate the importance of the IT audit to the institution's sustainability and resilience.

3. Lack of training and skills

- **Problem**: Employees may lack IT audit training and skills, limiting their ability to carry out effective audits.

- **Solution**: Offer ongoing training programmes to develop IT auditing skills. Encourage employees to obtain recognised professional certifications, such as Certified Information Systems Auditor (CISA).

4. Resistance to change

- **Problem**: Employees may resist IT audit initiatives due to fear of the unknown or apprehension about changes in their responsibilities.
- **Solution**: Involve employees from the outset of IT audit initiatives and encourage them to participate actively in the process. Recognise and reward positive contributions to motivate employees to embrace change.

5. Ineffective communication

- **Problem**: Ineffective communication can lead to a lack of clarity about the objectives and expectations of the IT audit.
- **Solution**: Set up clear and regular communication channels to inform employees of the progress, results and next steps of IT audits. Use a variety of communication media, such as meetings, newsletters and online platforms.

Conclusion

Awareness of IT audit is essential to ensure the success of audit initiatives and the security of MFIs' information systems. By investing in training, communication and employee engagement, microfinance institutions can overcome the challenges associated with lack of awareness and reap the full benefits of IT audit. A proactive and inclusive approach is the key to building a culture of IT audit awareness within the organisation.

Although IT audit presents challenges and limitations, it remains an essential tool for improving the security, efficiency and compliance of microfinance institutions. By proactively addressing these challenges and investing in the necessary resources, MFIs can overcome the obstacles and reap the full benefits of IT auditing. The key to success lies in awareness, training and commitment at all levels of the organisation.

CHAPTER 5: OUTLOOK AND RECOMMENDATIONS FOR THE FUTURE

5.1 Technological innovations and their potential impact on microfinance

Technological advances, such as mobile banking, blockchain and artificial intelligence, have the potential to transform the microfinance sector. These technologies can improve operational efficiency, reduce costs, and increase access to financial services for underserved populations. MFIs need to explore and embrace these innovations to remain competitive and relevant.

Technological innovations have the potential to radically transform the microfinance sector, making financial services more accessible and affordable for disadvantaged populations.[3] Here are some of the main technological innovations and their potential impact on microfinance:

1. Mobile Banking[4]

- **Impact**: Mobile banking allows customers to manage their finances via their mobile phones, even in the absence of traditional banking services. This increases financial inclusion by enabling people living in rural or remote areas to access financial services2.
- **Example**: Mobile payment solutions and e-wallets enable customers to make secure and rapid transactions.

2. Alternative Credit Scoring

- **Impact**: Alternative credit scoring methods use non-traditional data, such as psychometric data or mobile data, to assess customer creditworthiness. This makes it possible to include people with no formal credit history in the financial system2.
- **Example**: Psychometric tests and mobile data analysis to assess borrower credibility.

3. Bank by Agent

- **Impact**: Agent banking uses local traders as intermediaries to provide banking services in areas without bank branches. This extends the reach of financial services and reduces operational costs2.
- **Example**: Bank agents using point-of-sale (POS) terminals to process customers' financial transactions.

4. Biometric recognition

- **Impact**: Biometric recognition, such as fingerprint recognition, improves the security of financial transactions and enables customers to access their accounts securely.
- **Example**: POS terminals equipped with biometric scanners to authenticate customers.

---

[3] ifsa-network.com

[4] finca.org

5. Crowdfunding and personal loans[5]

- **Impact**: Crowdfunding and peer-to-peer lending enable micro-entrepreneurs to raise funds directly from the public, without going through traditional financial institutions.
- **Example**: Participative financing platforms that connect borrowers with potential investors.

6. Blockchain and Smart Contracts

- **Impact**: Blockchain technology and smart contracts can improve the transparency, security and efficiency of financial transactions by eliminating intermediaries and automating contracts.
- **Example**: Secure and transparent financial transactions using smart contracts on a blockchain.

These technological innovations have the potential to revolutionise microfinance by making financial services more accessible, secure and efficient for disadvantaged populations[6] . By adopting these technologies, microfinance institutions can better meet the needs of their customers and contribute to poverty reduction.

5.2 Strategies to enhance the effectiveness of IT auditing

Improving the effectiveness of IT audit is crucial for microfinance institutions to ensure the security, compliance and optimisation of their information systems. Here are some strategies for achieving this:

1. **Investment in audit tools and technologies**: MFIs should invest in modern audit tools and technologies to improve the accuracy and efficiency of their IT audits.

   - **Audit Management Tools**: Use audit management software such as ACL, IDEA or Teammate to automate and facilitate the management of the audit process.

   - **Security Monitoring Tools**: Implement monitoring solutions such as Splunk or SIEM to detect and analyse suspicious activity in real time.

   - **Vulnerability analysis**: Use tools such as Nessus or QualysGuard to scan systems and identify potential security flaws.

2. **Training and skills development**: It is essential to train staff in IT audit best practice and develop their skills to ensure they are capable of carrying out rigorous and comprehensive audits.

[5] link.springer.com
[6] link.springer.com

- **Ongoing training programme**: offering regular training to auditors to develop their technical skills and keep them up to date with the latest trends in security and auditing.

- **Professional certifications**: Encourage employees to obtain recognised certifications such as CISA (Certified Information Systems Auditor) or CISSP (Certified Information Systems Security Professional).

3. **Collaboration with external experts**: MFIs can benefit from the expertise of external IT auditors to carry out independent and impartial audits. These experts can provide fresh perspectives and recommendations based on industry best practice.

   - **Security standards**: Adopt international security standards such as ISO 27001 to structure and improve security practices.

   - **Audit Frameworks**: Use established audit frameworks such as COBIT (Control Objectives for Information and Related Technologies) to guide the audit process and ensure a structured approach.

5.3 Recommendations for microfinance institutions

1. **Strengthen governance and risk management**: MFIs need to put in place robust governance structures and risk management processes to ensure that information systems are secure and comply with regulations.

   Strengthening governance and risk management is crucial for microfinance institutions (MFIs) to ensure the stability, transparency and resilience of their operations. Here are some strategies for achieving this:

   1. Establishing sound governance

- **Governance structure**: Create a clear governance structure with defined roles and responsibilities for the Board, management and risk management committees.
- **Policies and Procedures**: Establish robust governance policies and procedures, including codes of conduct, conflict of interest policies and decision-making guidelines.
- **Transparency**: Promoting transparency by publishing regular financial reports and communicating clearly and openly with stakeholders.

   2. Risk Identification and Assessment

- **Risk mapping**: Carry out risk mapping to identify the main risks to which the institution is exposed, including financial, operational, market and reputational risks.
- **Risk assessment**: Use risk assessment methods to determine the probability and impact of each risk identified. Classify risks according to their criticality.

3. Setting up internal controls

- **Security Controls**: Implementing security controls to protect information systems against cyber-attacks and unauthorised access. This includes measures such as multi-factor authentication, firewalls and intrusion detection systems.
- **Financial Controls**: Establishing financial controls to ensure the accuracy and reliability of financial information. This includes transaction verification procedures, internal audits and compliance controls.

4. Business Continuity Management

- **Business Continuity Plan**: Develop a business continuity plan to ensure that the institution can continue to operate in the event of a major disruption. This plan should include data backup procedures, disaster recovery plans and emergency communication strategies.
- **Continuity tests**: Carry out regular continuity tests to ensure that contingency plans are effective and that staff are well prepared to react in the event of a crisis.

5. Training and awareness-raising

- **Employee training**: Offering training programmes to make employees aware of risks and teach them how to recognise and manage risky situations. This includes training on IT security, regulatory compliance and financial risk management.
- **Risk Culture**: Promoting an organisational culture that values proactive risk management and encourages employees to report problems and propose solutions.

6. Ongoing monitoring and evaluation

- **Risk Monitoring**: Implement continuous monitoring mechanisms to detect emerging risks and assess the effectiveness of internal controls. Use analysis and reporting tools to monitor key risk indicators.
- **Review and Improvement**: Regularly review risk management policies and procedures to ensure they are up to date and effective. Incorporate lessons learned and best practices to continuously improve the risk management framework.

By adopting these strategies, microfinance institutions can strengthen their governance and risk management, ensuring their resilience, transparency and ability to respond to future challenges. Strong governance and proactive risk management are essential to ensure the sustainability and success of MFIs in a constantly changing environment.

2. **Adopt a customer-centric approach**: MFIs need to design their financial services with their customers' needs and preferences in mind. This includes offering adapted products, simplifying processes and improving the user experience.

   For microfinance institutions (MFIs), adopting a customer-centric approach is essential to ensuring customer satisfaction and loyalty. This means understanding customers' needs, expectations and preferences, and designing appropriate financial products and services. Here are some strategies for adopting a customer-centric approach:

1. Knowing and Understanding Customers

- **Customer segmentation**: Segment customers into distinct groups based on their demographic, behavioural and financial characteristics. This provides a better understanding of the specific needs of each segment.
- **Surveys and Market Research**: Carrying out surveys and market research to gather information on customer expectations and preferences. Use this information to adapt products and services.

2. Development of Custom Products

- **Customised offerings**: Designing financial products and services that meet the specific needs of each customer segment. For example, micro-loans for entrepreneurs, savings accounts for farmers, etc.
- **Product innovation**: Innovating by developing new financial products that respond to the unique challenges faced by customers. For example, low-interest loans for women entrepreneurs or insurance tailored to small farmers.

3. Improving the Customer Experience

- **Quality Customer Service**: Implement a responsive, quality customer service. Train staff to actively listen to customers, answer their questions and resolve their problems quickly.
- **Multiple Communication Channels**: Offer several communication channels, such as physical branches, online services, mobile applications and call centres, so that customers can choose the channel that suits them best.

4. Financial education

- **Financial Education Programmes**: Setting up financial education programmes to help customers understand and manage their finances. This can include workshops, online training and information brochures.
- **Product Awareness**: Informing customers about the different financial products and services available, and helping them to choose those that best meet their needs.

5. Collecting and analysing feedback

- **Satisfaction assessment**: Use satisfaction surveys and customer feedback to assess customer satisfaction and identify areas for improvement.
- **Data analysis**: Analyse the data collected to detect trends and recurring problems. Use this information to improve products and services.

6. Customer loyalty

- **Loyalty programmes**: Set up loyalty programmes to reward loyal customers. This can include discounts, exclusive benefits and special events.
- **Personalised follow-up**: Maintain personalised follow-up of customers using customer relationship management (CRM) systems. Send follow-up messages, reminders and personalised offers to keep customers engaged.

7. Community involvement

- **Community involvement**: Actively participating in community life by supporting local initiatives and working with community organisations. This strengthens customers' trust in and attachment to the institution.
- **Social Responsibility**: Demonstrating a commitment to social responsibility by implementing projects and programmes that have a positive impact on the community.

By adopting these strategies, microfinance institutions can create an exceptional customer experience, build customer loyalty and strengthen their market position. A customer-centric approach is essential to meet customers' needs and contribute to their economic and social development.

3. **Promoting financial inclusion**: MFIs must continue to focus on financial inclusion by reaching unserved populations, particularly in rural areas and among marginalised groups. The use of technology can play a key role in this mission.

Financial inclusion is about ensuring that individuals and businesses have access to useful and affordable financial products and services that meet their needs. Here are some strategies for promoting financial inclusion within microfinance institutions (MFIs):

1. Development of Adapted Financial Products

- **Microcredit products**: Offering small loans tailored to the needs of micro-entrepreneurs and low-income households. These loans can help finance income-generating activities and unexpected expenses.
- **Savings Accounts**: Offering accessible and flexible savings accounts to encourage regular and secure savings among the unbanked.
- **Inclusive Insurance**: Developing affordable insurance products to protect customers against risks such as illness, accidents and natural disasters.

2. Use of Innovative Technologies

- **Mobile Banking**: Using mobile technologies to offer remote financial services, enabling customers to carry out transactions, deposit money and repay loans via their mobile phones.
- **Electronic wallets**: Promote the use of electronic wallets to facilitate digital payments and money transfers, thereby reducing reliance on cash transactions.
- **Payment Technologies**: Adopting innovative payment technologies such as QR codes and prepaid cards to offer secure and convenient payment solutions.

3. **Financial education and awareness**

- **Training programmes**: Set up financial training programmes to educate customers about money management, savings, responsible borrowing and the use of financial services.
- **Workshops and seminars**: Organise community workshops and seminars to raise awareness of the benefits of financial inclusion and encourage people to use formal financial services.

4. **Working with local partners**

- **Strategic Partnerships**: Working with NGOs, local associations, cooperatives and community organisations to reach underserved populations and promote financial inclusion.
- **Banking Agents**: Using local banking agents to offer financial services in rural and remote areas, where access to traditional bank branches is limited.

5. **Favourable Policies and Regulations**

- **Regulatory framework**: Working with regulators to develop a favourable regulatory framework that encourages financial inclusion, protects consumers' rights and guarantees the security of financial transactions.
- **Payment infrastructures**: Supporting the development of accessible and interoperable payment infrastructures to facilitate financial transactions between different institutions and platforms.

6. **Monitoring and evaluation**

- **Performance indicators**: Define performance indicators to measure the impact of financial inclusion initiatives and assess their effectiveness.
- **Customer feedback**: Gather regular feedback from customers to understand their needs, identify barriers to financial inclusion and adapt strategies accordingly.

By adopting these strategies, microfinance institutions can promote financial inclusion and contribute to improving the living conditions of disadvantaged populations. Access to appropriate and affordable financial services is essential for economic and social development, and for poverty reduction.

4. **Ongoing monitoring and evaluation**: MFIs must put in place monitoring and evaluation mechanisms to ensure that recommendations resulting from IT audits are implemented and that security and efficiency objectives are achieved.

Ongoing monitoring and evaluation are essential to ensure the effectiveness and continuous improvement of processes and initiatives within microfinance institutions (MFIs). Here are some strategies for implementing effective monitoring and evaluation:

1. Defining Performance Indicators

- Key Performance Indicators (KPIs): Identify and define specific KPIs to measure the performance of the various processes and initiatives. These indicators must be relevant, measurable and aligned with the institution's strategic objectives.
- SMART objectives: Use the SMART (Specific, Measurable, Achievable, Realistic, Time-bound) methodology to define clear, achievable objectives.

2. Data Collection

- Data Management Systems: Putting in place data management systems to collect, store and analyse data systematically and securely.
- Automation tools: Using automation tools to facilitate real-time data collection and reduce human error. Technologies such as the IoT (Internet of Things) can be used to collect data from a variety of sources.

3. Data analysis

- Quantitative analysis: Using quantitative analysis methods to assess performance and identify trends. Business intelligence tools and data analytics software can be used for this purpose.
- Qualitative analysis: Complementing quantitative analysis with qualitative methods such as interviews, surveys and focus groups to gain a deeper understanding of the issues and opportunities.

4. Reports and Feedback

- Regular reporting: Produce regular reports on performance, results and progress against objectives. These reports must be clear, concise and accessible to the various stakeholders.
- Constructive Feedback: Encourage constructive feedback from employees, customers and other stakeholders to identify areas for improvement and best practice.

5. Review and adjustment

- Periodic Reviews: Conduct periodic reviews of policies, procedures and initiatives to ensure they remain relevant and effective. Internal audits can be used to assess process compliance and effectiveness.
- Continuous improvement: Adopt a continuous improvement approach, using the results of analyses and feedback to adjust and improve processes and initiatives. Use methodologies such as the PDCA cycle (Plan-Do-Check-Act) to structure improvement efforts.

6. Commitment of Stakeholders

- Inclusion and Participation: Actively involve stakeholders in the monitoring and evaluation process. This includes employees, customers, regulators and local partners.
- Transparency: Ensure transparency in the communication of results and actions taken to improve performance. Stakeholders must be informed of progress made and challenges encountered.

7. Use of Advanced Technologies

- Big Data and Analytics: Exploiting big data and analytics technologies to analyse large quantities of data and gain valuable insights. This enables you to make informed decisions based on factual data.
- Artificial Intelligence (AI): Using AI and machine learning to predict trends, identify risks and optimise processes. These technologies can automate analysis tasks and provide data-driven recommendations.

By implementing these strategies, microfinance institutions can effectively monitor and evaluate their initiatives, continuously improve their processes and ensure their long-term success. Ongoing monitoring and evaluation enables them to remain agile and responsive to market challenges and opportunities, while ensuring transparency and accountability to stakeholders.

Conclusion

The future of microfinance lies in the ability of MFIs to innovate and adapt to technological developments and the changing needs of their clients. By investing in IT audit and adopting proactive strategies, MFIs can build resilience, improve performance and continue to play a crucial role in economic development and financial inclusion. The recommendations presented in this chapter provide a framework to guide MFIs towards a prosperous and sustainable future.

GENERAL CONCLUSION

1. Summary of key points discussed

In this book, we have explored various aspects of the impact of IT audit in microfinance institutions:

- **Chapter 1: Microfinance and its Importance**: We have discussed the history and evolution of microfinance, its main players and the challenges and opportunities it presents for economic development.
- **Chapter 2: IT Audit: Concepts and Methodologies**: We have defined the IT audit, its objectives, the different methods used, and the tools and techniques employed in the audit process.
- **Chapter 3: The Impact of IT Audit on Microfinance Operations**: We examined how IT audit can enhance data security, improve business processes, ensure regulatory compliance and manage risk. A case study was presented to illustrate these impacts.
- **Chapter 4: Challenges and Limitations of IT Audit in Microfinance**: We have identified the main challenges and limitations, such as costs, resistance to change, technical problems and the complexity of information systems.
- **Chapter 5: Perspectives and Recommendations for the Future**: We have discussed technological innovations and their potential impact on microfinance, strategies for strengthening the effectiveness of IT audit and recommendations for microfinance institutions.

2. Continued importance of IT audit for the security and efficiency of microfinance institutions

The IT audit remains an essential tool for microfinance institutions. It plays a crucial role in protecting sensitive data, managing risk and improving operational efficiency. By adopting robust audit practices, MFIs can guarantee the security of their information systems and ensure compliance with current regulations. In addition, an IT audit can identify inefficiencies and bottlenecks, making it easier to optimise processes and reduce costs.

In conclusion, an IT audit is essential for microfinance institutions wishing to maintain their competitiveness, strengthen the confidence of their customers and contribute to sustainable economic development. By investing in regular audits and adopting the recommendations arising from these assessments, MFIs can not only improve their performance, but also play a key role in financial inclusion and poverty reduction.

Appendices and References

1. Glossary of technical terms

- **IT audit**: Systematic process of gathering, analysing and evaluating evidence concerning an organisation's information systems and technological infrastructures.
- **Microfinance**: Financial sector that provides financial services to people on low incomes or excluded from traditional banking systems.
- **Systems security**: Protection of information systems against cyber-attacks, unauthorised access and data breaches.

- **Risk management**: Process of identifying, assessing and managing the risks associated with information technology.
- **Regulatory compliance**: Compliance with laws, regulations and internal policies on data protection and IT security.
- **Data integrity**: Accuracy, completeness and reliability of data processed by information systems.
- **Operational efficiency**: Performance of IT systems and processes, including their speed, availability and ability to meet the organisation's needs.
- **Penetration testing (Pentest)**: Simulation of attacks on systems to assess security and identify vulnerabilities.
- **Vulnerability analysis**: Assessment of systems and networks to identify security vulnerabilities.
- **Disaster recovery plan**: Measures required to guarantee continuity of operations in the event of a disaster or major breakdown.

2. Bibliography and sources used

- Yunus, M. (1999). **Bank of the poor**. Paris: JC Lattès.
- Ledgerwood, J. (1999). **Microfinance Handbook: An Institutional and Financial Perspective**. Washington, D.C.: The World Bank.
- Morduch, J., & Armendáriz de Aghion, B. (2010). **The Economics of Microfinance**. Cambridge, MA: MIT Press.
- Schreiner, M., & Colombet, H. H. (2001). **From Urban to Rural: Lessons for Microfinance from Argentina**. Development Policy Review, 19(3), 339-354.
- Lapenu, C., & Zeller, M. (2001). **Distribution, Growth, and Performance of Microfinance Institutions in Africa, Asia, and Latin America**. IFPRI FCND Discussion Paper No. 114.
- Deloitte (2020). **Guide to IT Auditing**. Wiley.
- ISACA. (2014). **COBIT 5: A Business Framework for the Governance and Management of Enterprise IT**.
- Stallings, W. (2017). **Cryptography and Network Security: Principles and Practice**. Pearson.
- Tipton, H. F., & Krause, M. (Eds.). (2012). **Information Security Management Handbook**. Auerbach Publications.

These resources provide in-depth information and varied perspectives on the subjects of microfinance, IT audit and information systems management. They can serve as a basis for further knowledge and research in these areas.

Table of contents

More Books!
yes

MIX
Papier aus verantwortungsvollen Quellen
Paper from responsible sources
FSC® C105338

Printed by Books on Demand GmbH, Norderstedt / Germany